ALROY'S

VERY NEARLY CLEAN BEDROOM

Wendy Orr   Illustrated by Bettina Guthridge

sundance

SUPa
DOOPERS

For information regarding permission, write to:
Sundance Publishing
234 Taylor Street
Littleton, MA   01460

Published by
Sundance Publishing
234 Taylor Street
Littleton, MA   01460

Copyright © text Wendy Orr
Copyright © illustrations Bettina Guthridge
Project commissioned and managed by
Lorraine Bambrough-Kelly, The Writer's Style
Cover and text design by Marta White

First published 1996 by
Addison Wesley Longman Australia Pty Limited
95 Coventry Street
South Melbourne 3205 Australia
Exclusive United States Distribution: Sundance Publishing

ISBN 0-7608-0763-9

PRINTED IN CANADA

Contents

Chapter 1   In Alroy's Bedroom   5

Chapter 2   Ready!   35

Chapter 3   What's That Noise?   51

Chapter 1

In Alroy's Bedroom

Alroy was in the jungle. He crawled under the hanging vines, through a tunnel, and up a steep, steep mountain. His toes found holes and his fingers found cracks; he pulled and wiggled and climbed to the top.

Far down below, a lion strode across the plains. It saw Alroy. It ran and jumped onto the low mountain beside Alroy's mountain. With a roar, it jumped towards him. Alroy reached for the lion . . .

and Alroy and the lion and the mountain crashed
down . . . down . . . down . . .

from the sky to the plains.

"Alroy!" shouted his mother.
"Are you cleaning your bedroom?"

"Yes," yelled Alroy.

Which was very nearly true, because he would as soon as he had crawled out from under the mountain. And now there were the clothes that had been vines, the bookcase-mountain, the books, the boomerang, the football and catcher's mitt, the wire-and-string crane and wooden planes, and all the other things from the shelves, as well.

Alroy picked up the bookcase first.

But when it was turned over, it looked like a
boat. A boat with rows of seats for lots of rowers.

Alroy put the rowers in place. He gave them
their oars and cracked a long whip. The lion on
the shore ran away, but a wolf came and howled
at the ship. The rowers cried for help, but Alroy
shouted at the wolf and cracked his whip again.

The wolf grabbed the end of his whip and pulled as hard as it could.

Alroy stood in his ship and pulled the other end as hard as *he* could.

The wolf let go and Alroy fell down.

The ship turned over, and the rowers were all thrown out.

Upside down, his boat looked like a raft.
Alroy climbed onto it.

He lay on the raft in the hot sun, but the raft
did not move. It needed a sail.

Alroy swam to shore and found a sail and a mast. He swam back to the raft with them.

He put up the mast and put the sail over it.

When it was night, he made the sail into a tent and went to sleep.

The lion swam out to the raft and came into the tent. It lay beside Alroy.

Suddenly the wolf rushed into the ocean,
swam across to the raft, and chased the lion.

The lion roared and Alroy yelled. The wolf grabbed the sail and yanked it off the raft.

Alroy grabbed it back, but the wolf kept on going . . . and the sail ripped in half.

"Alroy!" shouted his mother. "What **are** you doing?"

"Nothing!" yelled Alroy.

Which was very nearly true because he didn't know what he was going to do now that he'd fallen off the raft and could see the upside-down bookcase with the chair on top, the sheet in two pieces, the chewed-up belt, the books, the boomerang, the football, the catcher's mitt, the wire-and-string crane and wooden planes, and all the other things from the shelves, as well as the glow-in-the-dark dinosaurs that had been rowers.

He'd mend the sheet. A stapler would do it.
The stapler was in his desk. Somewhere in his
desk.

He pulled out the first drawer and dumped it out on the floor. And the second and the third.

He made three big piles of interesting stuff. The stapler wasn't in any of them.

The fourth drawer was stuck. He pulled and yanked, but it would not open.

Alroy was a construction worker.
It was his job to move this part of the building.

His workers pulled and
shoved, but they could
not move it.

His drivers
used a crane
and tractors
and machines,
but they could
not move it.

Alroy put dynamite under it and lit the fuse
and **BANG!**

The building fell down.

"Alroy!" shouted his mother. "Is anything wrong in there?"

"No," yelled Alroy.

Which was very nearly true, except that now he'd moved the building, the desk was lying in the middle of the piles of things from the drawers, and everything else he'd knocked down before.

He tried to push the desk back up.

But he pushed the wrong way, and it crashed upside down.

Alroy was in a spaceship. The spaceship fired up,
roared, blasted off, and climbed higher and
higher into space.

Through his portholes, Alroy could see enemy
spaceships. They were going to attack!

Alroy got his missiles ready. He fired at the enemy spaceships. Some of the missiles landed **SPLATT!** on their targets, but he needed more.

More and more missiles — he was going to win.

A space wolf flew past his rocket. It rushed at
the missiles and caught one of them. Alroy
blasted another missile, and the monster leapt
onto a soft white planet and caught *it* instead
of the missile.

The soft white planet exploded and filled the
universe with a snowstorm. The space wolf
yelped and blasted back to Earth.

Chapter 2

Ready!

"Alroy!" shouted his mother. "We're leaving for Great Gran's birthday party in fifteen minutes. If you haven't finished cleaning your room . . ."

"I'm almost finished!" yelled Alroy.

Which was very nearly true, except for the bookcase and books, the boomerang, the football, the catcher's mitt, the wire-and-string crane and wooden planes, and all the other things from the shelves; the clothes, the sheet in two pieces, the chewed-up belt, and the chair; the desk and piles of things from the drawers; the missiles, and the pillowcase and feathers from the pillow. And a few other things that had been on the floor before he started.

"Fourteen minutes!" shouted his mother. "And don't forget to change!"

Alroy pulled off his shorts and his T-shirt.
He found his favorite hat and tried it on.
He looked in the wardrobe for a long time, and
then he shook the feathers off his jeans and took
a nearly clean T-shirt he found under the
feathers and put them on.

Under the bed he found some socks and his
favorite sneakers.

"Five minutes!" shouted his mother.

Alroy picked up the chair and stood it up.
He heaved the desk up and pushed it
against the wall. He shoved the three empty
drawers back into his desk.

He opened the closet. He kicked in the clothes and the boomerang, the football, the catcher's mitt, the glow-in-the-dark dinosaurs, the crane made of wire and string and the wooden planes. He pushed in the sheet and the pillow and feathers. He shoved in the sketch pads, screwdrivers, electric buzzer kits, and all the other things from the drawers. He squeezed in the rock collection, the egg-in-a-bottle-experiment, and the other things that had been on the floor when he started.

Then he stacked all the books on top, shut the door as fast as he could . . . and pushed the bookcase in front of it before it could open again.

"Alroy!" shouted his mother. "It's time to go! Are you ready?"

"Ready!" yelled Alroy.
Which was exactly true, because after all that cleaning he was extremely ready to get out of his room.

His great gran's birthday wasn't really a party.
There was just a cake and presents and talking.

They talked about Great Gran's birthday plant and where she was going to put it in her kitchen, about the book Grandad had given her and the movie they were going to see next week. Alroy wasn't allowed to watch television because they were talking. He couldn't go outside because there was no garden.

He couldn't do anything because there was nothing to do.

Alroy tried to be lost on an island in the middle of the ocean, but their talk floated over the water.

"Nothing exciting ever happens to me!"
Alroy muttered, and his grandad laughed and
messed up his hair.

It was late when they got home.
"Alroy," said his mother, "I told you to turn off
your bedroom light before we left."
"I did," said Alroy.

Chapter 3

What's That Noise?

They went into the house.
"Straight to bed, Alroy," said his mother.
And then . . . "What's that noise?"

It was a very strange noise. Like someone yelling
in his sleep or having a nightmare. Or shouting
from the end of a very long tunnel.

Or a burglar calling "Help!" from the bottom of a mountain of books, rocks, dinosaurs, feathers, wire-and-string cranes, egg-in-a-bottle-experiments, and everything else that could possibly be in a bedroom.

Alroy stared, his father yelled, and his mother phoned the police.

Two police cars screamed up the driveway with their sirens howling and lights flashing, and the two policemen raced inside.

"Where is the burglar?" they shouted.

And then they saw where he was, and they dug some of Alroy's room off him.

"What happened?" they asked.

"When I saw that bookcase in front of the door," the burglar moaned, "I thought there must be computers or jewelry or a video hidden inside.

But when I opened it, I got buried in an avalanche!

I'm never going to break into a house again!"

"Not in prison, you won't," said the policeman, putting the handcuffs on.

"Alroy," said his mother, "I thought you said
your bedroom was tidy."

"It was," said Alroy. "But then I thought since we were going out, it would be a good idea to set a burglar trap."

Which was very nearly true...

Wendy Orr

Wendy Orr grew up in many different places across Canada, France, and the United States. She studied occupational therapy in England, and while she was there married an Australian farmer. She now lives on a dairy farm in Victoria and has two children, two dogs, and a cat. Wendy has written many books for children and teenagers and has won official awards from the Children's Book Council of Australia.

About the Illustrator

Bettina Guthridge

Bettina went to art school in Melbourne and lived and worked in Italy for ten years. She has two children and a dog called Tex. Her first picture book was *Matilda and the Dragon,* and she has since illustrated many books for children by Australian authors Margaret Clark and Sally Morgan, American author Ogden Nash, and British author Roald Dahl.

In 1995, Bettina had her own exhibition of found object sculptures at Melbourne's Yume Ya Gallery.